Russian Ly

CW00656181

Translator: Martha Dickinson Bianchi

Alpha Editions

This edition published in 2023

ISBN : 9789357939485

Design and Setting By
Alpha Editions
www.alphaedis.com
Email - info@alphaedis.com

To the Reader.

The translations in this little collection make no pretension to being more than an effort to share the delight found in them; from which most of the world is debarred by the difficulty of the language in which they are written. They have been chosen at random, each for some intrinsic charm or because of its bearing upon some peculiar phase of the author. Very few of the lyrics of Pushkin have been included, for the reason that the great founder of Russian poetry has been more widely translated than any other Russian poet, and is therefore available in several languages.

Remembering always that Heine declared translation was betrayal,—the rhyme and smoothness have in every case been sacrificed when necessary to preserve the exact rhythm, and as far as possible the vigour and colour, as well as thought of the original; a task entirely beyond me save for the co-operation of an accomplished Russian linguist who has kindly assisted in the literal translation of every poem here presented.

M.G.D.B.

THE SONG OF THE KAZAK

Kazak speeds ever toward the North,
  Kazak has never heart for rest,
Not on the field, nor in the wood,
  Nor when in face of danger pressed
His steed the raging stream must breast!

Kazak speeds ever toward the North,
With him a mighty power brings,
To win the honour of his land
  Kazak his life unheeding flings—
Till fame of him eternal sings!

Kazak brought all Siberia
At foot of Russia's throne to lie,
Kazak left glory in the Alps,
  His name the Turk can terrify,
His flag he ever carries high!

Kazak speeds ever toward the North,
Kazak has never heart for rest,
Not on the field, nor in the wood,
  Nor when in face of danger pressed
His steed the raging stream must breast!

PUSHKIN.

The accent in singing falls sharply on the second half—Kazák.

CRADLE SONG OF A COSSACK MOTHER

Slumber sweet, my fairest baby,
  Slumber calmly, sleep—
Peaceful moonbeams light thy chamber,
  In thy cradle creep;
I will tell to thee a story,
  Pure as dewdrop glow,
Close those two beloved eyelids—
  Lullaby, By-low!

List! The Terek o'er its pebbles
  Blusters through the vale,
On its shores the little Khirgez
  Whets his murdrous blade;

Yet thy father grey in battle—
  Guards thee, child of woe,
Safely rest thee in thy cradle,
  Lullaby, By-low!

Grievous times will sure befall thee,
  Danger, slaughterous fire—
Thou shalt on a charger gallop,
  Curbing at desire;
And a saddle girth all silken
  Sadly I will sew,
Slumber now my wide-eyed darling,
  Lullaby, By-low!

When I see thee, my own Being,
  As a Cossack true,
Must I only convoy give thee—
  "Mother dear, adieu!"
Nightly in the empty chamber
  Blinding tears will flow,
Sleep my angel, sweetest dear one,
  Lullaby, By-low!

Thy return I'll wait lamenting
  As the days go by,
Ardent for thee praying,—fearing
  In the cards to spy.
I shall fancy thou wilt suffer,
  As a stranger grow—
Sleep while yet thou nought regrettest,
  Lullaby, By-low!

I will send a holy image
  'Gainst the foe with thee,
To it kneeling, dearest Being,
  Pray with piety!
Think of me in bloody battle,
  Dearest child of woe,
Slumber soft within thy cradle,
  Lullaby, By-low!

LERMONTOFF.

THE DAGGER

I love thee dagger mine, thou sure defence—
  I love the beauty of thy glitter cold,
A brooding Georgian whetted thee for war,
  Forged for revenge thou wert by Khirgez bold.

A lily hand, in parting's silent woe,
  Gave thee to me in morning's twilight shade;
Instead of blood, I saw thee first be-dewed
  With sorrow's tear-pearls flowing o'er thy blade.

Two dusky eyes so true and pure of soul,
  Mute in the throe of love's mysterious pain—
Like thine own steel within the fire's glow,
  Flashed forth to me—then faded dull again.

For a soul-pledge thou wert by love appointed,
  In my life's night to guide me to my end;
Stedfast and true my heart shall be forever,
  Like thee, like thee, my steely hearted friend!

LERMONTOFF.

DON'T GIVE ME THE WINE!

Don't give me the wine!
                    I am drunk of my love,
With the force of my passion for you!
Don't give me the wine!
                    Or my tongue will betray
All the love no one dreamed hitherto;
For wine will reveal all I hid in my breast,
All the bitter hot tears that were mine,
My thirst, without hope, for a future so blest—
I am drunk of my love,—don't give me the wine!

You promise me roses now, if I will drink
But one drop of the wine;—if you please
Give only one breath from the rose of your lips!
And death's cup I will drain to the lees.
All passions are raging at once in my blood,
Know my frenzy! Love's madness is mine.
You seem for my suffering only to wish—

I am drunk of my love!

             Don't give me the wine!

From the Georgian of Prince Tschawtschawadze.

THE DELIBASH

With the hostile camp in skirmish
   Our men once were changing shot,
Pranced the Delibash his charger
   'Fore our ranks of Cossacks hot.

Trifle not with free-born Cossacks!
   Nor too o'er foolhardy be!
Thy mad mood thou wilt atone for—
   On his pike he'll skewer thee!

'Ware friend Cossack! Or at full bound,
   Off thy head, at lightning speed
With his scimitar he'll sever
   From thy trunk! He will indeed!

What confusion! What a roaring!
   Halt! thou devil's pack, have care!
On the pike is lanced the horseman—
   Headless stands the Cossack there!

PUSHKIN.

Delibash is the Turkish synonym for Hotspur.

TO THE DON

Through the Steppes, see there he glances!
   Silent flood glad hailed by me,—
Thy far distant sons do proffer
   Through me, greeting fond to thee!

Every stream knows thee as brother,
   Don, thou river boasted wide!
The Araxes and Euphrates
   Send thee greeting as they glide.

Fresh and strengthened for pursuing,
   Scenting home within thy gleam—

Drink again the Don'ish horses,
   Flowing boundary, of thy stream!

Faithful Don! There also greet thee
   Thy true warriors bold and free—
Let thy vineyard's foaming bubbles
   In the glass be spilled to thee!

PUSHKIN.

The valley of the Don is the home of the Russian Cossack.

THE CAUCAS

The Caucas lies before my feet! I stand where
   Glaciers gleam, beside a precipice rock-ribbed;
An eagle that has soared from off some distant cliff,
Lawless as I, sweeps through the radiant air!
Here I see streams at their sources up-welling,
The grim avalanches unrolling and swelling!

The soft cloudy convoys are stretched forth below,
Tattered by thronging mad torrents descending;
Beneath them the naked rocks downward are bending,
Still deeper, the wild shrubs and sparse herbage grow;
But yonder the forests stand verdant in flora
And birds are a'twitter in choiring chorus.

Yonder, cliff-nested-are dwellings of mortals,
There pasture the lambs in sweet blossoming meadows—
There couch the herds in the cool deepening shadows—
There roar the Aragua's blue sparkling waters,
And lurketh the bandit safe hid in lone caverns,
Where Terek, wild sporting, is cutting the azure!

It leaps and it howls like some ravening beast
At first sight of feeding, through grating of iron—
It roars on the shore with a furious purring,
It licks on the pebbles with eagerest greed.
Vain struggle and rancor and hatred, alas!
'Tis enchained and subdued by the unheeding mass.

PUSHKIN.

THE CLOISTER ON KASBEK

KASBEK, thy regal canopy
   High o'er all peaks revealed I see
By an eternal icy glare.
Hanging in cloudless glory ever—
Like to an ark thy cloister there;
This world disturbing thy peace never,
Blest realm of joy remote in air!
Ah could I at thy mercy's threshold,
From durance cursed set myself free,
And in thine own etherial cloisters
Near thy Creator ever be!

PUSHKIN.

GOBLINS OP THE STEPPES

Stormy clouds delirious straying,
Showers of whirling snowflakes white,
And the pallid moonbeams waning—
Sad the heavens, sad the night!
Further speeds the sledge, and further,
Loud the sleighbell's melody,
Grewsome, frightful 'tis becoming,
'Mid these snow fields now to be!

Hasten! "That is useless, Master,
Heavier for my team their load,
And my eyes with snow o'er plastered
Can no longer see the road!
Lost all trace of our direction,
Sir, what now? The goblins draw
Us already round in circles,
Pull the sledge with evil claw!

See! One hops with frantic gesture,
In my face to grin and hiss,
See! It goads the frenzied horses
Onward to the black abyss!
In the darkness, like a paling
One stands forth,—and now I see
Him like walking-fire sparkling—
Then the blackness,—woe is me!"

Stormy clouds delirious straying,
Showers of snowflakes whirling white,
And the pallid moonbeams waning—
Sad the heavens, sad the night!
Sudden halt the weary horses,
Silent too the sleighbells whirr—
Look! What crouches on the ground there?
"Wolf,—or shrub,—I know not, Sir."

How the wind's brood rage and whimper!
Scenting, blow the triple team;
See! One hops here! Forward Driver!
How his eyes with evil gleam!
Scarce controllable the horses,
How the harness bells resound!
Look! With what a sneering grimace
Now the spirit band surround!

In an endless long procession,
Formless, countless of their kind
Circle us in flying coveys
Like the leaves in Autumn wind.
Now in ghastly silence deathly,
Now with shrilling elfin cry—
Is it some mad dance of bridal,
Or a death march passing by?

Stormy clouds delirious straying
Showers of snowflakes whirling white,
And the pallid moonbeams waning—
Sad the heavens, sad the night!
Cloudward course the evil spirits
In unceasing phantom bands,
And their moaning and bewailing
Grip my heart with icy hands!

PUSHKIN.

UNDER A PORTRAIT OF JUKOWSKY

The charm and sweetness of his magic verse
   Will mock the envious years for centuries!
Since youth, on hearing them, for glory burns,
   The wordless sorrow comfort in them sees,
And careless joy to wistful musing turns.

PUSHKIN.

Jukowsky was a Russian poet.

THE VISION

I remember a marvellous instant,
Unto me bending down from above,
Thy radiant vision appearing
As an angel of beauty and love.
'Mid the torments of desperate sadness,
In the torture of bondage and sighs,
To me rang thy voice so beloved—
And I dreamed thy miraculous eyes.
But the years rolled along—and life's tempests
My illusions, my youth overcame,
I forgot that sweet voice full of music—
And thy glance like a heavenly flame.
In the covert and grief of my exile,
The days stretched unchanged in their flight,
Bereft inspiration or power,
Bereft both of love and of light.
To my soul now approaches awakening,
To me thou art come from above,
As a radiant and wonderful vision—
As an angel of beauty and love.
As before my heart throbs with emotion,
Life looks to me worthy and bright,
And I feel inspiration and power—
And again love and tears and the light!

PUSHKIN.

I LOVED THEE

I loved thee; and perchance until this moment
Within my breast is smouldering still the fire!
Yet I would spare thy pain the least renewal,
Nothing shall rouse again the old desire!

I loved thee with a silent desperation—
Now timid, now with jealousy brought low,

I loved devoutly,—with such deep devotion—
Ah may God grant another love thee so!

PUSHKIN.

A SERENADE

I watch Inesilla
  Thy window beneath,
Deep slumbers the villa
  In night's dusky sheath.

Enamoured I linger,
  Close mantled, for thee—
With sword and with guitar,
  O look once on me!

Art sleeping? Wilt wake thee
  Guitar tones so light?
The argus-eyed greybeard
  My swift sword shall smite.

The ladder of ropes
  Throw me fearlessly now!
Dost falter? Hast thou, Sweet,
  Been false to thy vow?

I watch Inesilla
  Thy window beneath,
Deep slumbers the villa
  In night's dusky sheath!

PUSHKIN.

A WINTER EVENING

Sable clouds by tempest driven,
Snowflakes whirling in the gales,
Hark—it sounds like grim wolves howling,
Hark—now like a child it wails!
Creeping through the rustling straw thatch,
Rattling on the mortared walls,
Like some weary wanderer knocking—
On the lowly pane it falls.

Fearsome darkness fills the kitchen,
Drear and lonely our retreat,
Speak a word and break the silence,
Dearest little Mother, sweet!
Has the moaning of the tempest
Closed thine eyelids wearily?
Has the spinning wheel's soft whirring
Hummed a cradle song to thee?

Sweetheart of my youthful Springtime,
Thou true-souled companion dear—
Let us drink! Away with sadness!
Wine will fill our hearts with cheer.
Sing the song how free and careless
Birds live in a distant land—
Sing the song of maids at morning
Meeting by the brook's clear strand!

Sable clouds by tempest driven,
Snowflakes whirling in the gales,
Hark—it sounds like grim wolves howling,
Hark—now like a child it wails!
Sweetheart of my youthful Springtime,
Thou true-souled companion dear,
Let us drink! Away with sadness!
Wine will fill our hearts with cheer!

PUSHKIN.

THE LAST FLOWER

Rich the first flower's graces be,
But dearer far the last to me;
My spirit feels renewal sweet,
Of all my dreams hope or desire—
The hours of parting oft inspire
More than the moments when we meet!

PUSHKIN.

THE COMING OF THE WINTER

Stanzas from "Onegin"

Our Northern Winter's fickle Summer,
Than Southern Winter scarce more bland—
Is undeniably withdrawing
On fleeting footsteps from the land.
Soon will the Autumn dim the heavens,
The light of sunbeams rarer grown—
Already every day is shorter,
While with a smitten hollow tone
The forest drops its shadow leafage;
Upon the fields the mists lie white,
In lusty caravans the wild geese
Now to the milder South take flight;
Seasons of tedium draw near,
Before the door November drear!

From shivering mist ascends the morning,
The bustle, of the fields declines,
The wolf walks now upon the highway,
In wolfish hunger howls and whines;
The traveller's pony scents him, snorting—
The heedful wanderer breathless takes
His way in haste beyond the mountains!
And though no longer when day breaks
Forth from their stalls the herd begins
To drive the kine,—his noon-day horn recalls.
The peasant maiden sings and spins,
Before her crackling, flaming bright
The pine chips,—friend of Winter night.

And see! The hoar frost colder sparkles
And spreads its silver o'er the fields,
Alas! the golden days are vanished!
Reluctant Nature mournful yields.
The stream with ice all frozen over
Gleams as some fashionable parquét,
And thronging hordes of boyish skaters
Sweep forward on its crystal way.
On her red claws despondent swimming,
The plump goose parts the water cold,
Then on the ice with caution stalking
She slips and tumbles,—ah behold!
Now the first snowflake idling down
Stars the depressing landscape brown.

At such a season in the country,
What can a man's amusements be?
Walk? And but more of empty highway
And of deserted village see?
Or let him through the far Steppes gallop,
His horse can scarcely stand at all—
His stamping hoofs in vain seek foothold,
The rider dreading lest he fall!
So then remain within thy paling,
Read thou in Pradt or Walter Scott,
Compare thy varying editions,
Drink, and thy scoffing mood spare not!
As the long evenings drag away
So doth the Winter too delay.

PUSHKIN.

[Pradt was a French political writer, Minister to the Grand Duchy of Warsaw in 1812. Nine editions of his History of the Embassy at Warsaw were demanded.]

FROM "ONEGIN"

Sometimes he read aloud with Olga
A latter day romance discreet,
Whose author truly painted nature,
With cunning plot, insight complete;
Oft he passed over a few pages,
Too bald or tasteless in their art—
And coloring, began on further,
Not to disturb the maiden heart.
Again, they sat for hours together,
With but a chess board to divide;
She with her arms propped on the table,
Deep pondering, puzzled to decide—
Till Lenski from his inward storm
Captured her castle with his pawn!

PUSHKIN.

FROM "ONEGIN"

Love condescends to every altar,
Ah when in hearts of youth it springs,

Its coming brings such glad refreshment
As May rain o'er the pasture flings!
Lifted from passion's melancholy
The life breaks forth in fairer flower,
The soul receives a new enrichment—
Fruition sweet and full of power.
But when on later altars arid
It downward sweeps, about us flows—
Love leaves behind such deathly traces
As Autumn tempests where it blows
To strip the woods with ruthless hand,
And turn to soggy waste the land!

PUSHKIN.

FROM "ONEGIN"

How sad to me is thine appearing,
O Springtime, hour of love's unrest!
Within the soul what nameless languors!
What passions hid within the breast!
With what a heavy, heavy spirit
From the earth's rustic lap I feel
Again the joy of Springtide odors—
That once could make my spirit reel!
No more for me such pleasures thrilling,
All that rejoices, that has life,
All that exults,—brings but despondence
To one past passion as past strife,
All is but prose to such as he,
Wearied unto satiety.

Perchance we fain would pass unnoticed
That which in Autumn drooped and pined,
Now radiant in verdure springing,
Since it must of our loss remind;
As with a tortured soul we realize
In Nature's glad awakening,
That we shall never find renewal,
Who evermore are withering.
Perchance there haunts us in remembrance,
Our own most dear and lyric dream,
Another long forgotten Springtime—

And trembling neath this pang supreme,
The heart faints for a distant country
And for a night beside the sea!

PUSHKIN.

THE MEMORIAL

Beyond compare the monument I have erected,
And to this spirit column well-worn the people's path,—
Its head defiant will out-soar that famous pillar
  The Emperor Alexander hath!

I shall not vanish wholly,—No! but young forever
My spirit will live on, within my lyre will ring,
And men within this world shall hold me in remembrance
  While yet one Singer lives to sing.

My glory shall in future fly through distant Russia,
Each race in its own tongue shall name me far and wide,
The Slav, the Finn, the Kalmyk, all shall know me—
  The Tungoose in his reindeer hide.

Among my people I shall be long loved and cherished,
Because their noblest instincts I have e'er inflamed,
In evil hours I lit their hearts with fires of freedom,
  And never for their pleasures blamed.

O Muse, pursue the calling of thy Gods forever!
Strive not for the garland, nor look upon the pain—
Unmoved support the voice of scorn or of laudation,
  And argument with Fools disdain!

PUSHKIN.

The Alexander column, standing before the Winter Palace at St. Petersburg, is a monolith eighty feet high; with the pedestal measuring one hundred and fifty feet.

TAMARA

Where waves of the Terek are waltzing
  In Dariel's wickedest pass,
There rises from bleakest of storm crags
  An ancient grey towering mass.

In this tower by mad winds assaulted,
  Sat ever Tamara, the Queen—
A heavenly angel of beauty,
  With a spirit of hell's own demesne.

Through the mist of the night her gold fires
  Gleamed down through the valley below,
A welcome they threw to the pilgrim,
  In their streaming and beckoning glow.

How clear rang the voice of Tamara!
  How amorous did it invite!
The heart of the stranger enticing,
  Seducing with magic delight!

The warrior was snared by her singing,
  Nor noble, nor herd could withstand—
Then noiseless her portal was opened
  By eunuchs of shadowy hand.

With pearls rare adorned and strange jewels,
  Reposed on a billowy nest,
A prey to voluptuous longing,
  Tamara awaited her guest.

With passioned and thrilling embracement,
  With straining of breast unto breast,
With sighing and trembling and transport—
  In lust's unrestrained, giddy zest—

So revelled 'mid desolate ruins,
  Of Lovers,—past counting at least!
In their bridal night's wild distraction,
  And in truth at their own death feast.

For when from the peaks of the mountains
  The sun tore the night's veiling soft,
There reigned anew only the silence
  On turret and casement aloft.

And only the Terek bewailing
  With fury broke in on the hush,
As dashing her billows on billows
  Her writhing floods onward did rush.

A youth's form her currents are bearing,
  Ah vainly they murmur and swell!

A woman, a pale and a fair one—
  Cries down from her tower "Farewell!"

Her voice has the sound of faint weeping,
  So amorous, tender and sweet—
As if she in love's holy rapture
  Did promise of meeting repeat!

LERMONTOFF.

[*Tamara is the Russian Lorelei. The ruins of her castle are still shown in the pass of Darjal on the famous Georgian Road.*]

THE GIFT OF THE TEREK

Through the rocks in wildest courses
  Seethes the Terek grim of mood,
Tempest howling its bewailing,
  Pearled with foam its tearful flood.

At the mountain's feet soft streaming,
  Gentler grown its murmurs be,
And with greeting full of fawning
  Speaks to the Caspian Sea:

"Hospitable part thy billows,
  Give me room, oh Ocean grave!
From a distance drawing thither—
  Scarce my weary currents wave.

Born upon the edge of Kasbek,
  By the breast of clouds renewed,
Hatred have I sworn to mankind,
  Who with us, the free, make feud.

See, by rage of my own fury
  Lies despoiled my Darjal home,
And as playthings for thy children,
  Pebbles bearing now I come."

Yet upon her strands a'dreaming,
  Mute the grey Sea did remain,
And the Terek, silver foaming,
  Spoke caressingly again.

"Grey Sea I would serve thee only,
  Have a present borne to-day—

See, 'tis a young Carabineer
  Who has fallen in the fray.

How his coat of mail is gleaming
  Silver on the billows' span!
Golden on his trappings shining
  Blessing of the Alcoran!

Menacing the one who slew him
  Scowls the brow's relentless feud,
By his noble life blood crimsoned
  O'er his lips his hair is glued.

Through the half-closed eyelids glancing
  Still the lust of quarrel mocks,
From his head deep underneath him
  Flow the matted raven locks."

Motionless upon her beaches
  Did the grey Sea still remain,
And the Terek foaming yellow
  In displeasure spoke again.

"So then, take him as a present,
  As I nothing fairer know
On this round earth,—for thee only
  This rare prize I've guarded so!

'Tis a mountain Cossack's body
  Wafted 'mid my billows' dance,
See his hair,—no silk is softer—
  See his shoulder's gold expanse!

See how o'er his red lips speechless
  Now the seated eyes find rest;
Trickling yet the purple life blood
  From the small wound on his breast.

For a young and holy maiden,
  Weeps lamenting, every heart!
One sole Cossack in the village,
  In this mourning takes no part.

From the confines of his country
  Rode he forth with boding grey,
'Neath the dagger of the Tscherkes
  He has breathed his soul away."

And the Terek paused; behold now
  In the gleaming foam flood drowned,
Silvered in the spraying billows
  Dips a head with rushes crowned.

And the hoary one's lips whisper
  Haughty words of youthful fire,
And the eyes lit with love lustre
  Flame with passionate desire.

Foaming, rushing on swift longing,
  Seethed he up in youthful zest—
And the Terek flood was wedded
  With him in embraces blest.

LERMONTOFF.

ON DEPARTURE FOR THE CAUCAS

Farewell my hateful Russian country!
  People of lord and serf you are—
Farewell, salute, bent knee and hand-kiss,
  Three-masters, uniform and star!

Soon will the Caucas now conceal me,
  There I shall not discovered be
By eyes and ears of paid, false sergeants—
  Who all do hear and all do see!

LERMONTOFF.

TO THE CLOUDS

Clouds—ye eternal wanderers in hunting grounds of air,
High o'er the verdant Steppes, wide through the blue of heaven—
Coursing fraternal,—say, must ye exiled as I
From the beloved North to the far South be driven?

O tell me, were ye outlawed thus by Fate's behest?
Drives ye forth open hate, or secret grudge flee ye?
Follows ye unappeased an evil-doer's curse?
Are ye pursued by poisonous words of calumny?

Ah no! Only from the unfruitful earth ye fly;
Free are your sufferings, your blessedness is free,

Ye know not wretchedness that holds us here in chains,
Know not the joy of home or exile's misery!

LERMONTOFF.

TO MY COUNTRY

With love of my own race I cling unto my country,
Whatever dubious reason may protesting cry;
The shame alone of all her blood bought glory,
Her haughty self-assurance, conscious pride,
And the ancestral faith's traditions dark,
With woe have penetrated all my heart.

And yet I love it! Why, I cannot say;
The endless snowy Steppes so silent brooding,
In the pine forests Autumn winds pursuing—
The flood's high water on all sides in May.
By peasant cart I fain would haste in nightly darkness,
Through the lone wilderness and village desolate,
How hospitable shines the sole beam sparkling
To me from each poor hut! Filled with content so great,
The smell of stubble burnt, delights. Piled high
The wagons silent standing take their nightly rest,
On distant hills the silver birches I descry,
Framed gold by fertile fields the sacred picture blest.
Then with a joy unshared save by the vagrant,
I see the threshing floor well filled and fragrant,
The sloping straw-thatched cottage roofs again,
The window panels carved, of varied stain.

Nightly could I, till morning grey arrested,
Gaze on the dancing, stamping, whistling crowd,
Watching the villager,—young, happy, festive—
And hearing drunken peasants glad carouse!

LERMONTOFF.

TO KASBEK

With wingéd footsteps now I hasten
Unto the far cold North away,
Kasbek,—thou watchman of the East,
To thee, my farewell greetings say!

Since all eternity, a turban
Snow white, thy glorious brow has veiled,
The peace sublime about thy glacier
The strife of man has ne'er assailed.

Accept my humble supplication,
Hear thy submissive faithful son,
To starry heights lift his entreaty
To Allah's everlasting throne.

I do implore—spice breathing coolness
Through sultry sun-glow in the vale,
A stone for rest unto the pilgrim
In whirling dust of desert gale.

Turn, I implore, the storm's hot hatred,
The deadly thunderous lightning's course—
In Dariel's wild pass protect me
And my distracted, trembling horse.

Yet one prayer more my heart audacious,
Weeping, lifts up in bodeful stress,
What if my native land forget me
In my sad exile's loneliness?

Will, greeting me by name familiar,
My friend then open wide his arms?
Will e'en my brothers recognise me,
So changed by many griefs and harms?

Perchance my foot will fall profaning
Dust of those loved in youth's far day,
The pure and noble, deeply trusted—
Withered as Autumn leaves in May.

O Kasbek, then with earth o'erwhelm me!
Snow o'er thy weary wanderer back,
And blow away my dust and scatter
Along thy rock-ridged clefts lone track!

LERMONTOFF.

THE ANGEL

Soft singing at midnight through heaven's high blue
  A beautiful angel once flew;

The moon and the stars and the clouds in a throng
  Attended his wonderful song!

He sang of the bliss of those gardens and coasts
  Where live and exult the pure ghosts,
Their songs glad extolling Almighty's grace
  Repeated from race unto race.

In his arms he was bearing a young soul below,
  To leave in this world of our woe,
The strains of his singing within her soul beat—
  A wordless song, living and sweet!

Long languished her soul in its earthly abode,
  With a heavenly longing o'erflowed,
For ne'er were those holy, pure strains of her birth,
  Effaced by the songs of the earth.

LERMONTOFF.

A PRAYER

Faithful before thee, Mother of God, now kneeling,
Image miraculous and merciful—of thee
Not for my soul's health nor battles waged, beseeching,
Nor yet with thanks or penitence o'erwhelming me!

Not for myself,—my heart with guilt o'erflowing—
Who in my home land e'er a stranger has remained,
No, a sinless child upon thy mercy throwing,
That thou protect her innocence unstained!

Worthy the highest bliss, with happiness O bless her!
Grant her a friend to stand unchanging at her side,
A youth of sunshine and an old age tranquil,
A spirit where together peace and hope abide.

Then, when strikes the hour her way from earth for wending,
Let her heart break at dawning or at dead of night—
From out thy highest heaven, thy fairest angel sending
The fairest of all souls sustain in heavenward flight!

LERMONTOFF.

THE SAIL

A single sail is bleaching brightly
  Upon the waves caressing bland,
What seeks it in a stranger country?
  Why did it leave its native strand?
When winds pipe high, load roar the billows
  And with a crashing bends the mast,
It does not shun its luckless fortune,
  Nor haste to port before the blast.
To-day the sea is clear as azure,
  The sun shines gaily, faint the wind—
But it revolting, looks for tempest,
  And dreams in storms its peace to find!

LERMONTOFF.

Lermontoff, being reproached by the critics of his time for imitation of Byron in this poem, defended himself by the following, "I am not Byron!"

I AM NOT BYRON

I am not Byron—yet I am
One fore-elected, yet one more
Unknown, world-hunted wanderer,
A Russian in my mood and mind.

Scant from my seed the corn was ripe,
My mouth spoke young, was early hushed;
In depths of my own soul, the wreck
Of hope lies as in deep-sea sunk.

Who shall the counsels of the sea,
Its awe sublime unloose? Who shall
Read clear my spirit and my soul?
Unless it be a Poet—no man!

LERMONTOFF.

LIKE AN EVIL SPIRIT

Like an evil spirit hast thou
  Shocked my heart from out its rest,
If thou'lt take it quite away now—
  Thou wilt win my healing blest!

My heart thy temple evermore!
  Thy face,—the altar's Godhead sign!
Not heaven's grace,—thy smiles, restore,
  Grant absolution, joy divine!

LERMONTOFF.

TO A.C.S.

Afar—I fain, so much would tell thee!
List to thee o'er and o'er when near;
Yet passioned glances thou dost silence—
My words bind to my lips in fear.
How, by mere homely speaking, can I
E'en hope to captivate thine ears?
I swear it would be food for laughter—
If it were not more fit for tears!

LERMONTOFF.

A SONG

Dry leaf trembling on the branches
  Before the blast,
Poor heart quaking in the bosom
  For woe thou hast;
Ah what matter if the wind then,
  Withered leaf from blooming linden
Should scatter wide?
  Would for this the twig or branches
    Have wailing sighed?
And should the lad his fate upbraid,
  Although he ignominious fade—
And in an alien country die?
  Will for him the beauteous maid
    Complaining cry?

LERMONTOFF.

FROM "DÉMON"

Sailless and without a rudder,
  On the ocean of the air—

Float the choirs of stars harmonious,
  'Mid the mists eternal there;
Fleecy flocks of clouds elusive
  Drift across immensity,
Leaving ne'er a track behind them,
  Following their destiny.
Hour of parting, hour of meeting
  They know not,—nor grief, nor rest—
Theirs no longing for the future,
  Theirs no sorrow for the past.
By thy day of anguish broken,
  Think of them and calm thy woe—
Be indifferent as they are
  To the pangs of earth below!

LERMONTOFF.

THE PRAYER

When faints the heart for sorrow,
  In life's hard, darkened hour,
My spirit breathes a wondrous prayer
  Full of love's inward power.

There is a might inspiring
  Each consecrated word,
That speaks the inconceivable
  And holy will of God.

The heavy load slips from my heart—
  Oppressing doubt takes flight,
The soul believes, the tears break forth—
  And all is light, so light!

LERMONTOFF.

THE PALM BRANCH OF PALESTINE

Palm branch of Palestine, oh tell me,
  In that far distant home-land fair,
Wast rooted in the mountain gravel
  Or sprung from some vale garden rare?

Once o'er the Jordan's silver billows
  Fond kissed with thee the Eastern sun?
Have the grim gales 'neath starry heavens
  Swept over thee from Lebanon?

And was a trembling prayer soft whispered,
  A father's song sung over thee—
When from the parent stem dis-severed
  By some poor aborigine?

And is the palm tree ever standing,
  Amid the fierce glare beating down,
The pilgrim in the desert luring
  To shelter 'neath her shadow crown?

Perhaps the leaves ancestral shiver
In unappeaséd parting pain,
The branch conceals a homesick longing
  For desert wilderness again?

Was it a pilgrim who first brought thee
  To the cold North, with pious hand?
Who mused upon his home in sadness,
  And dost thou bear his tear's hot brand?

Was it Jehovah's favored warrior,
  His gleaming head transfigured bright,
For God and man true-sworn, devoted
  Unto the victory of light?

Before the wonder-working image
  Thou stand'st as heaven's defence divine,
O branch from out that holy country,
  The sanctuary's shield and sign!

It darkens, golden lamp light splendors
  Enveil the cross, the sacred shrine—
The peace of God is wafted o'er us
  From thee, oh branch of Palestine!

LERMONTOFF.

THE DISPUTE

Once 'mid group of native mountains
  Hot dispute arose,
Elbrus, angry, did with Kasbek

Argument propose.
"Now beware!" the hoary Elbrus,
  Warning did exclaim—
"To enslave thee and enthrall thee
  Is man's evil aim!
Smoking huts he will be building
  On thy mountain side,
Loudly through thy clefts resounding
  Ring his hatchet wide!
The swift swinging iron shovel
  Breast of stone will part,
Of thy bronze and stone will rob thee—
  Pierce thee to the heart.
Caravans, e'en now, are passing
  Through thy rocks afar,
Where before the fogs were swimming—
  And the Eagle Tsar.
Ah, mankind is bold and fearless!
  Dreads no lifted hand,
Guard thee! populous and mighty
  Is the morning land!"
"Threatens me the East?" then queried
  Kasbek with disdain,
"There eight centuries already
  Sleeping, man has lain.
See, in shadow the Grusine
  Gloats in lustful greed,
On his many coloured raiment
  Glints the winey bead!
Drugged with fumes of his nargileh,
  Dreams the Mussulman—
By the fountains on his divan
  Slumbers Teheran.
See! Jerusalem is lying
  At his feet o'erthrown—
Deathly dumb and lifeless staring
  As an earthly tomb.
And beyond the Nile is washing
  O'er the burning steps
Of the Kingly mausoleums,
  Yellow, shadowless.
In his tent, the hunt forgotten—
  Now the Bedouin lies,

Sings the old ancestral legends,
　Scans the starry skies.
See! far as the eye can venture,
　All sleeps as before—
No, the threat of dreaming Orient
　Frights me nevermore!"
"Laugh thou not too early, Kasbek,"
　Elbrus did persist—
"Look! What vast mass is it turning
　Northward, through the mist?"
Secretly the heart of Kasbek
　Faltered,—as amazed,
Silent and with dark foreboding
　To the North he gazed:
Full of woe stared in the distance;
　What a thronging swarm!
Hark! there rings the clash of weapons!
　Battle-cry alarm!
From the Don unto the Ural
　What a human sea!
Regiments that wave and glitter
　Past all counting be!
Feathers white like sedge of ocean,
　Waving in a gust—
Many coloured Uhlans storming
　Through the blowing dust.
The imperial battalions
　Densely packed proceed,
Trumpets flaring, banners flying
　In the victor's lead.
Batteries with brasses rattling
　Conquering advance,
With their blood-red splendor flashing
　Cannon matches glance.
And a battle-proved commander
　Leads the army there—
From whose eyes the lightning flashes,
　'Neath his snowy hair.
Swells the host until as Griesbach's
　Billows roaring loud,
From the Eastward nears the army
　As a thunder cloud.
Kasbek peered with sinister boding

Through the clouds,—would fain
Count his enemies approaching—
  Found it was in vain:
Threw one glance unto the mountains—
  Anguished, overcome,
O'er his brow drew close the vapours,
  Was forever dumb.

LERMONTOFF.

HEAVEN AND THE STARS

Brilliant heavens of evening,
  Distant stars clearly shining,
  Bright as the rapture of childhood,
O why dare I send you nevermore greeting—
Stars, who are shining as clear as my joy?
  What is thy sorrow?
  Mortals make question.
  This is my sorrow;
The heavens and the stars are—heaven and stars ever,
I am alas! but a perishing man!
  Forever mortal
  Envies his neighbor;
  I envy rather
Ye in your freedom, ye stars ever radiant,
And only would be in your places!

LERMONTOFF.

ON NAPOLEON'S DEATH

Cold hears thy soul the praise or cursing of posterity.
Quit of the human race, thou man of destiny!
They only could o'erthrow, who thee did elevate—
Forever thus remains thy greatness great!

LERMONTOFF.

ON THE DEATH OF PUSHKIN

He fell, a slave of tinsel-honour,
A sacrifice to slander's lust;

The haughty Poet's head, the noblest,
Bowed on his wounded breast in dust.
No longer could his free soul suffer
The vulgar world's low infamy;
He rose against the world's opinion,
And as a hero, lone fell he.
He fell! To what avail the sobbing—
The useless choir of tears and praise?
Wretched the stammering excuses!
The Fates have spoke,—no power allays!
Have ye not at all times together
His sacred genius baited sore,
The silent fury fanned to flaming,
Delighted in your work before?
O be triumphant! Earthly torment
The Poet soul did fully bear,
Extinguished are the lights inspired,
The laurel crown lies leafless there!
The murderer contemptuous gazing
Did stedfastly his weapon aim,
No swifter beat his heart, Assassin!
Nor shook his lifted hand for shame.
No wonder; from a distance came he
As an adventurer unknown,
For worthy title, star of order—
Stood but his mad desire alone.
Sneering and self-complacent mocked he
The rights and customs of our land,
He could not understand our glory,
Against which he has raised his hand.

"Hence is he, hence! His song out-rung,
The Singer even as the song he sung;
Who of a hot, heroic mood,
In death disgraceful shed his blood!"[1]

Why did he leave his home life tranquil,
To seek the envious market place,
Where each free flame is suffocated,
Expose him to the assassin base?
The human breed, who had known better
Since earliest years of youth, than he—
Why did he trust the false pretending
Of malice and hypocrisy?

Ah, of his laurel wreath you robbed him,
Gave him a martyr's crown instead,
And now the cruel thorns have pierced him
E'en to the blood of his proud head!
His last days were for him envenomed—
Through senseless fools' contempt aggrieved,
He died revenge a'thirst, accusing
That every hope his heart deceived!

Mute evermore the magic echoes,
That ne'er shall wonders more reveal,
The Poet's home is dark and narrow—
Upon the Singer's lips a seal.

But ye, sons insolent and shameless—
Defamers, faithless fathers, ye!
Who trod the pure soul of another
Beneath your feet, who zealously
Press to the Tsar's throne with your driveling
For fame and freedom, hatred steeled!
Well may you sneer at truth and justice,
The law provides you screen and shield,
Only a higher law shall sentence!
A mighty Judge beyond assail
Avenge the Poet's death on his slayers,
The Highest Judge who does not fail!
So then calumniate with brazen courage,
Your hatred's fury nought restrains—
Since your dark blood could ne'er atone for
One drop within the Poet's pure veins.

LERMONTOFF. [1] *These four lines are from Pushkin's own romantic poem,*
"Onegin."

RUSSIA, O MY RUSSIA, HAIL!

Russia, O my Russia, hail!
Steeds as tempests flying,
Howling of the distant wolves,
Eagles high, shrill crying!
Hail, my Russia, hail! Hail high!
Hail thy green forests proud,
Hail thy silvery nightingales,
Hail Steppes and wind and cloud!

TOLSTOY.

THE WOLVES

When the church-village slumbers
  And the last songs are sung,
When the grey mist arising,
  Is o'er the marshes hung,
'Tis then the woods forsaking,
Their way cross country taking,
Nine howling wolves come hungering for food.

Behind the first,—the grey one,—
  Trot seven more of black,
Close on their hoary leader;
  As rearguard of the pack
The red wolf limps, all bloody,
His paws with gore still ruddy
As after his companions grim he pants.

When through the village lurking
  Nought gives them check or fright,
No watch dog dares to bellow,
  The peasant ghastly white,
His breath can scarce be taking,
His limbs withhold from shaking—
While prayers of terror freeze upon his lips!

About the church they circle
  And softly slink away
To prowl about the priest's farm,
  Then of a sudden they
Are round the drink shop turning,
Fain some bad word be learning—
From peasants drinking noisily within.

With fully thirteen bullets
  Thy weapon must be armed,
And with a wad of goat's hair;
  Then thou wilt fight unharmed.
Fire calmly,—and before all
Will the leader, the grey, fall,
The rest will surely follow one by one.

When the cock wakes the village
From out its morning dream,
Thou wilt behold the corpses—
Nine she-wolves by the stream!
On the right lies the grey one,
To left in frost the lame one—
All bloody,—God pardon us sinners!

TOLSTOY.

AUTUMN

Autumn 'tis! Our garden stands
Flowerless and bare,
Dizzy whirling yellow leaves
Fill the wind swept air.
Yet the distant mountain ash
In the vale below,
With our favorite berries red
Now begins to glow.
While with rapture and with pain
Throbbing in my breast,
Pressing hot thy hands in mine,
Silent, unexpressed—
Fondly gazing in thine eyes,
Through my tears I see—
That I can never tell thee
How dear thou art to me!

TOLSTOY.

BURNT OUT IS NOW MY MISERY

Burnt out is now my misery—
love's yearning
No more unspeakably torments my heart,
Yet bearable alone through thee, my being—
All thou art not is idle, stale and dying,
Colourless, withered, dead,—save where thou art!

If I no more through false suspicion trouble
Thy happiness,—nor more my blood inflames my veins,
It is not turned to ice 'neath snowy cover,

But free from jealousy, to thee thy lover
Always with soul of ardour true remains.

So in their rapid fury mountain torrents
That hurl them off their moss-grown altars steep,
Seeking the flood with tossing, foaming riot—
Here in the vale are bound in the old currents,
To stream in future calm and clear and deep!

TOLSTOY.

IN HOURS OF EBBING TIDE

In hours of ebbing tide, oh trust not to the Sea!
  It will come back to shore with redness of the morrow;
  O don't believe in me when in the trance of sorrow
I swear I am no longer true to thee!

The waves will roll again in dazzling ecstasy,
  From far away, with joy, to the belovéd shore;
  And I with breast aflame, beneath thy charm once more,
Shall haste to bring my liberty to thee!

TOLSTOY.

SWANS

White Swans, ye harbingers of Spring, a greeting fond from me!
Rejoicing thrills within the breast of Mother Earth anew—
From her once more the flowers push forth 'mid gleaming drops of dew,
And like the Swans, across my soul my dreams will lightly sweep,
And my heart blissful throbbing, ghostly tears of rapture weep.
O Spring I feel thy coming! And behold Thee, Poesy!

MAIKOW.

TO SLEEP

When shadows pale are sinking in hues the twilight weaves,
Upon the golden grain fields of gleaming wheaten sheaves—
Upon the emerald pastures and blue of forests deep,
When the soft mists of silver o'er the sea doth creep;
When 'mid the reeds, the swan's head is pillowed 'neath her wings,
The stream to sleep is rocking, light flowing as she sings,—

Then to my hut o'er thatched with golden straw,—o'er grown
By frail acacia green and leafy oaks, I turn.
And there with greeting holy, in radiant starry crown—
Her scented locks with deepest of purple poppies bound,
And with one dusky gauze enveiled her snowy breast—
The Goddess comes to me with sweet desire of rest.
A faint and roseate fire about my brow she sheds,
Soft mystery of azure above my eyelids spreads,
Bends low upon my breast her regal star-crowned tresses
And on my mouth and eyes, the kiss of slumber presses!

MAIKOW.

IN MEMORY OF MY DAUGHTER

Clear on the night of my spirit,
To me shines the glance of a star,
It is she! My heart's little maiden!
From her glance gleams something afar,
Of victory, deathless, eternal—
Something that musing, misgiving,
Pierces the essence of being!

It cannot be! It cannot be!
She lives—soon she will waken; straightway
Will ope her pretty eyes,—glad she
Will prattle merry, laughing gay!
And when in tears beholding me—
Will smiling, kissing, cry consoling,
"Papa—it is but playing—See!
I live,—yes! Leave off mourning!"
   But cold and mute she lies, alas!
   And motionless.

Now in her coffin she lies,
Silent amid scented flowers—
Ah what mute spirits in white
O'er her corpse circle and hover?
Are they the visions of bliss?
Are they all spirits of hope?
That during life lured her on—

Those to whom secretly oft
She had entrusted her soul?
They that accompanied her e'er,

Faithful in forest and field?
Silent they circle my child,
In tearful anguish embraced—
Yet little actress she lies,
Smiling, closed lashes beneath;
See, she is laughing in truth—
thou most merciless Death!

MAIKOW.

MOTHER AND CHILD

"Mother, why weepest thou ever
   For my little sister fair?
She is now in heaven's kingdom—
   Ah, it must be wondrous there!"

"Yes, she is in heaven's glory,
   But in heaven's own land, alas!
There are no butterflies nor flowers—
   Nor meadows of velvet grass!"

"But mother, God's blessed angels
   There, rejoicing sing to Him!"
Forth from the sunset's rosy fires
   Now cometh the midnight dim.

Ah, the mother wants her baby—
   That she watched from the window wide,
When 'mid butterflies and blossoms
   She played in the meadow's pride!

MAIKOW.

AN EASTER GREETING

The lark at sunrise trills it high—
The greeting Christ is risen!
And through the wood the black-bird pipes
The greeting Christ is risen!
Beneath the eaves the swallows cry
The greeting Christ is risen!
Throughout the world man's heart proclaims
The greeting Christ is risen!

And echo answers from the grave
In truth, yes, He is risen!

MAIKOW.

AT EASTER

Drawing near the Easter Sunday
With the Easter-greeting kiss;
When I come, remember Dora—
Not alone we suffer this!
Then, as were it for the first time—
Kiss thou me and I kiss thee;
Thou with modest eyelids downcast,
I with but ill stifled glee!

MAIKOW.

The religious custom of the Easter-greeting kiss prevails throughout Russia.

O MOUNTAINS OF MY NATIVE COUNTRY!

"O mountains of my native country! O valleys of my home!
On you gleam Winter's snowflakes white and twinkle lambs of Summer—
On you the rosy sunlight glows, you know no deathly shudder!"

So, 'neath the earth did wistful yearn three homesick youths in Hades,
Who fain from out that under world to worlds above would hasten.
  The first declared "We'll go in Spring!" The second "No, in Summer!"
"No," cried the third, "at harvesting, in time the grapes to gather!"
A listening maiden fair, o'erheard with heart resistless throbbing;
Upon her breast her arms she crossed and begged of them imploring—
  "O take me to the upper world!" Alone the youths made answer,
"That cannot be, you fairest maid, that you with us be taken!
Your heels would clatter as you speed, your dress would rustle silken,
Your rattling ornaments warn death to hear us all escaping."

"My rustling dress I will unlace,—my ornaments forsaking,
Barefooted up the stairway steep will mute and cautious follow!
Ah, but too gladly would I gaze again on earthly living!
I fain my mother would console, sad for her daughter grieving—
would my brothers twain behold, who for their sister sorrow!"
  "O do not yearn, thou wretched child, for those thou lovest, ever!

Thy brothers in the village street now joyful lead the wrestling—
And with the neighbors on the street thy mother gossips zestful!"

MAIKOW.

THE AEOLIAN HARP

The land lies parched in sun,—to heaven the air is still,
Hushed now upon the harp the golden strings' lost thrill;
Aeolian harps our native singers are,—and numb
Must be their heart, their dying life blood cease to flow,
Forever silent be their voice, if longer dumb
Their breath be suffocated in this sultry glow!
O if a Genius on tempest-pinions winging,
Stormed through our native land,—Spirit with freedom rife!
How jubilant would our Aeolian harps be ringing
To greet the Godly power that promises new life!

MAIKOW.

YE SONGS OF MINE!

Ye songs of mine! Of universal sorrows
  A living witness ye;
Born of the passion of the soul, bewailing
  Tempestuous and free,
The hard heart of humanity assailing
  As doth her cliffs the sea!

NEKRASSOW.

IN WAR

Hearing the terrors of the war, sore troubled,
  By each new victim of the combat torn—
Nor friend, nor wife I give my utmost pity,
  Nor do I for the fallen hero mourn.
Alas! the wife will find a consolation.
  The friend by friend is soon forgot in turn.

But somewhere is the one soul that remembers—
  That will remember unto death's dark shore,
Nor can the tears of a heart-stricken mother

Forget the sons gone down on fields of gore.
One soul there is that like the weeping willow
  Can never raise its drooping branches more.

NEKRASSOW.

THE SONGS OF SIBERIAN EXILES

We stand unbroken in our places,
Our shovels dare to take no rest,
For not in vain his golden treasure
God buried deep in earth's dark breast.

Then shovel on and do not falter,
Humble and hopeful, clear we see—
When Russia has grown rich and mighty,
Our grandchildren will grateful be!

* * * * *

Though streams the sweat in rivers downward,
Our arms from shoveling grown weak,
Our bodies frozen to an ice crust
While we new strength in slumber seek—

Sweating or freezing, we will bear it!
Thirst-pain and hunger will withstand,
For each stone is of use to Russia,
And each is given by our own hand!

NEKRASSOW.

Written to a band of political exiles including some of the highest aristocracy.

FREEDOM

Oft through my native land I roved before,
But never such a cheerful spirit bore.

When on its mother's breast a child I spy—
Hope in my inmost heart doth secret cry,

"Boy, thou art born within a favoring time,
Thine eyes shall glad escape old sights of crime.

Free as a child, thou can'st prove all and be
The forger sole of thine own destiny.

Peasant remain,—as to thy father given—
Or like the eagle swing thyself to heaven!"

Castles in air I build! Man's spirit opes
To many ways to frustrate all my hopes.

Though serfdom's sad conditions left behind,
Yet there be countless snares of varied kind!—

Well! Although the people soon may rend thee,
Let me, oh Freedom, a welcome send thee!

NEKRASSOW.

Written shortly after the freeing of the serfs.

A FAREWELL

Farewell! Forget the days of trial,
Of grudge, ill humor, misery—
Tempests of heart and floods of weeping,
And the revengeful jealousy.
Ah, but the days whereon the sun rose
To light love's wonder, and begot
In us the power of aspiration,—
bless them and forget them not!

NEKRASSOW.

THE LOVE LETTER

Letter of love so strangely thrilling
With all your countless wonder yet,
Though Time our heart's hot fires have mastered,
Bringing a pang of pained regret!
The while your blest receiver holds you,
His banished passions still rebel,
No longer reason sacrifices
His sentiment,—so then farewell!
Destroyed be this love-token treasured!
For if 'tis read when time has flown,
Deep in the buried soul 'twill waken
The torment vanished days have known.
At first but a light scorn arousing
For silly childishness,—at last

With fiery yearning overwhelming,
And jealousy for all the past.

O Thou, from whom a myriad letters
Speak with the breath of love to me,
Though my gaze rest on thee austerely,
Yet, yet,—I cannot part with thee!
Time has revealed with bitter clearness
How little thou with truth wert blessed,
How like a child my own behaviour—
Yet, dear to me I still must save
This flower scentless, without colour,
From off my manhood's early grave!

NEKRASSOW.

WHAT THE SLEEPLESS GRANDAM THINKS

All through the cold night, beating wings shadowy
  Sweep o'er the church-village poor,—
Only one Grandam a hundred years hoary,
  Findeth her slumber no more.

Harkens, if cocks to the dawn be not crowing,
  Rolls on her oven and weeps,
Sees all her past rising up to confront her—
  O'er her soul shameful it creeps!

"Woe to me sinner old! Woe! Once I cheated—
  When from the church door I ran,
And in the depths of the forest strayed hidden
  With my beloved Ivan.

"Woe to me! Burning in hell's leaping fires
  Surely will soon be my soul!
I took a pair of eggs once at a neighbor's—
  Out from her hen—yes, I stole!

"Once at the harvest at home I did linger—
  Swore I was deadly sick,—when
Taking my part in the drunken carousals
  Saturday night with the men!

"Light was I ever with soldiers! Yet cursing
  God's name, when from me at last,—

My own son they took for a soldier!
  Even drank cream on a fast.

"Woe to me sinner! Woe to me wretched one!
  Woe! My heart broken will be!
Holy Madonna, have pity, have mercy!
  Into court go not with me!"

NEKRASSOW.

The stoves of the peasants are built so that they can sleep on top of them in the extreme cold of Winter.

TO RUSSIA

'Neath a giant tent
Of the heavens blue,
Stretch the verdant Steppes;
Range beyond the view.

On the distant rim
Lift the outlines proud,
Of their mountain walls
To the drifting cloud.

Through the Steppes there rolls
Stream on stream to sea,
Wide meandering,
Straying far and free.

Do I Southward gaze—
Like the ocean there,
Ripening fields of grain
Wave and ripple fair.

Softest velvet sod
Decks the meadow floor,
In the vineyards green
Swells the grape once more.

Do I Northward turn—
O'er the waste lands lone,
Soft as eider down
Are the snowflakes blown.

And his azure waves
High the ocean lifts,

On his cold blue breast
Now an iceberg drifts.

And as leaping flame
Burn the Northern lights,
On the darkness gleam
Through the silent nights.

Even so art thou,
Russian realm, become,—
Thou my native land,
Shield of Christendom!

Far away hast thou,
Throughout lands untold,
In thy glory fair,
Russia, been enrolled!

Art thou not in space
E'en o'er well supplied?
Where a spirit bold
Freely wanders wide!

Hast thou not alway
Gold and grain rich stored?
For thy friend a feast?
For thy foe a sword?

Guards and shields thee not
With a sacred might,
Holy altar forms,
Deeds of glory bright?

To whom hast thou e'er
Bent an humble knee?
Or before whom bowed
Seeking charity?

In the Kurgan deep,
Met in open fight,
Thou hast e'en subdued
The fierce Tartar's might.

Fought to bloody death
The Lithuanian horde,
The defiant Pole
Scattered with a sword.

And how long ago,
Black clouds, rising out
Of the distant West,
Compassed thee about?

'Neath the lightning flash
Sank the woods away,
Trembled the earth's breast,
Piercéd with dismay.

And the inky smoke
Ruinous did rise
From the village burnt
To the cloudy skies.

Loudly to the fight
Then the Tsar did call—
Russia swift replied,
Coming one and all.

Women, children came—
Men from age to youth,
Gave their evil guest
Bloody feast in truth!

And in lonely fields
Under ice and snow,
To his endless sleep
Laid the victim low.

Where the snowstorms wild
Raised o'er him a tomb,
While the North wind sang
Dirges in the gloom.

Town and village too
Over all our land,
Now like ant hills swarm
With this Christian band.

Now from distant shores
O'er the cruel sea,
Ship on ship draws near
Homage paying thee.

Blooming are thy fields,
Soft thy forests sigh,

Hid in earth's dark breast
Golden treasures lie.

And to East and West,
To the South and North—
Flies thy louder fame
Through the wide world forth!

Holy Russia, thou
Dost deserve to be
"Mother" called by all,
In our love to thee!

For thy glory fair
We should face the foe,
And thy freedom guarding
Glad our lives bestow!

NIKITIN.

THE SONG OP THE SPENDTHRIFT

To seven kopek the heir,
  Nor house nor land have I—
Live I—hey! I live then!
  Die I—hey! I die!

In many realms the Fool
  Can sleep no wink for care,
While yet the spendthrift snores
  When dawns the morning fair.

Free as the wind he blows,
  Door nor gate to balk him,
Riches, hey! Now give place!
  Poverty goes walking!

Before me bends the rye
  When through the fields I stray
And glad the forest hears
  My pipe and song alway.

If one must bitter weep—
  No man will see his tears,
If sadly bowed his head—
  None save the partridge jeers.

If weary one, or not,
    What matters anything?
Let him toss back his locks
    And playful laugh and sing!

And if one die,—the grave
    Will warm his hands and feet!
Dost to my song respond?
    Nay? Then it is complete.

NIKITIN.

THE SPADE IS DEEP DIGGING A GRAVE IN THE MOULD

The spade is deep digging a grave in the mould....
O Life,—so o'erflowing with sorrows untold,
My life, so homeless and lonely and weary,
Life, as an Autumn night silent and dreary—
Bitter in truth is thy fate 'neath the sky,
And as a fire of the field wilt thou die!
Die then—no sad falling tear will recall thee,
Fast will the roof of thy pine coffin wall thee,
Heavy the earth falls upon the sad hearted—
Only one more from humanity parted;
One whose home-going no fond heart is tearing—
One for whom no soul will sorrow despairing!

Hark! What a silvery music is ringing!
Hark! What a careless and jubilant singing!
See on ethereal azure waves swinging,
Now the glad lark to her South-land is winging!
Silence, O Life full of doubting and fears,
Hushed first of all be the songs of men's tears!

NIKITIN.

GOSSIP

Though blameless thy living
    As Anchorite's fate,
Yet Gossip will find thee
    Or early or late.

Through keyhole he enters
  And stands at thy side,
Doors of wood nor of stone
  Against him provide.

He pulls the alarm bell
  At slightest excuse—
And down to thy grave
  Will pursue with abuse.

Self defence nothing boots thee,
  Thy flight he will worst—
To earth he will tread thee,
  O Gossip be cursed!

NIKITIN.

IN A PEASANT HUT

Sultry dampness—pine chips smoking,
Off-scourings a span length,
In the corners webs of spiders,
Smut on dish and bench.

Sooty black the bare wall, crock stained,
Water—dry hard bread;
Groanings, coughings, children's whimper,
Wretched bitter need!

And a beggar's death for years of
Harshest drudgery—
Learn to put your trust in God here,
And to patient be.

NIKITIN.

WINTER NIGHT IN THE VILLAGE

O'er the church roof wanders
  Mute and calm the moon,
Blue upon the snowdrifts
  Sparkling silent down.

By the small pond dreaming,
  Stands the church a'gleam—

With its gold cross twinkling
  As a taper's beam.

Peaceful in the village
  Darkness reigns and sleep,
Every hut is standing
  Snowed in window deep.

Out upon the highway
  Hushed and empty all,
Now the howling watch dogs
  Even, silent fall.

After their day's labor
  Young and old are pressed
Weak and worn, on their hard
  Narrow place of rest.

In one cottage only
  Shines a lamplight, where
A sick old hoary-head
  Groans in soul-despair.

Death is near,—and of her
  Grandchildren thinks she,
Smitten sore the orphans
  Harvest time will be.

Ah the poor, poor children!
  Now so young for strife,
All untried and helpless
  In the woe of life!

Among stranger people
  Older they will grow—
Evil hearts will lure them
  Evil ways to go.

With disgrace too early
  They will make a bond,
Shamed and God forsaken
  Sink unto the ground.

Dear God, thyself take them,
  Thy forsaken poor—
Staff and light be to them
  Thyself evermore!

And the sacred lamplight
  Calm and silent strays;
On the holy pictures
  Fall its trembling rays;

O'er the aged features,
  O'er the dying form,
O'er the two small children
  On the stove bench warm.

Sudden, through the stillness
  Rings a merry cry—
And his jingling troika
  Drives a reveller by!

Dies in silent distance
  Sleighbell clangor strong,
And the careless, merry,
  Sorrow-troubling song.

NIKITIN.

THE BIRCH TREE

From bald and sun-parched earth it rises,
  One lonely birch, high towering—
Upon its withered crown wide spreading,
  Green leafage never more will sing.

Up to the rim of the horizon
  Where veiling mists all soft enclose,
Runneth the blossoming of flowers,
  The Steppe's green ocean waving flows.

In green enchantment stands the Kurgan,
  Where evening dampness doth enfold,
The night descends with sleep and coolness,
  The morning sunbeams touch with gold.

Yet loveless, helpless stands the birch tree—
  In heaven's grey, musing sad to view,
And from its branches fall like tear-drops
  The gleaming pearls of morning dew.

Scattered, alas! her tender leaflets,
  In howling storms,—so far, so wide!

Ne'er will the birch, to greet the Springtide,
  Be fresh adorned in leafy pride!

NIKITIN.

NORTH AND SOUTH

Knowest thou the land of fragrance ardent glowing?
Where night sublimely sparkles on the flowing
Of the sea? Murmuring in starlight gleam—
Weaving about the heart a wonder dream?
Refulgent in the silvering moonbeams white,
In soft half darkness, gardens slumbering light;
Only the fountain's iridescent foam
Upon the grass falls splashing down—
And images of Gods with lips of silence
Sunk in deep musing gaze on every side—
While, eloquent of fallen majesty,
Ruins entwined with ivy tendrils be?
Soft pictured on the valley's verdant meadows
Dark cypress trees reflect their slender shadows;
Earth's bosom blooming in fecundity—
And freedom here man's joyful destiny.

Yet more than tropic's soft abundance thralling,
My stormy North-land wilderness is calling!
Her snowflake flocks, her gleaming midnight frosts,
The glory of grim forests on her coasts,
Green tinted Steppes with distant bluish rim—
The trooping clouds in heaven's spaces dim.
Unto the heart how the familiar cries!
The village mean that in the valley lies,
The wealthy cities' towering majesty,
The empty snow-fields' endless boundary,—
The changeful moods that all unbridled throng;
Spirit of Russia and of Russian song!
With joy now gushing forth,—with pain now ringing—
Unto the hearer's heart resistless singing.

Thou fairest picture! my breast with rapture sighs,
My spirits free, victorious arise!
A song breaks forth to Russia's praise and glory,
And tears of joy, the while I muse, are flowing.

And jubilant the kindling heart must cry—
Hail Russia, Hail! Thy loyal son am I!

NIKITIN.

HUNGER

Hark! Who knocks with bony fingers
  On the hut's small window latch?
Hark! Who pulls away the stubble
  Rustling, from the roofing thatch?

From the fields it is not Vintage,
  Drunk and weary wavers home—
'Tis a spectre, meagre, gloomy,
  As a nightmare dread become.

All subduing, all destroying,
  In his ragged garment poor,
Drags he,—on his crutches limping—
  Noiseless reeling through the door.

Like the usurer hard hearted,
  For his last kopek in quest,
Coffer, cupboard both he opens,
  Breaks the lock of case and chest.

Lordly rules he, late and early—
  In the granary; when gone
Every kernel of provision,
  The last cattle he will pawn.

From the land unto the cellar,
  Clean the peasant's hut he keeps,
With a coarse and clumsy besom
  Every tiny crumb he sweeps.

On the village highway also
  Works and wins he over all,
From the threshing floor to stable—
  From the sheepfold to the stall.

His approaching, sorrow follows—
  On his coming, follows need,
On his greeting, follows sickness,
  On his hand-shake Death succeeds!

So he seeks in all directions,
   East and West and South and North—
And in empty field embraces
   Thankfully his friend the Frost!

FOFANOW.

FADED THE FOOTSTEP OF SPRING FROM OUR GARDEN

Faded the footstep of Spring from our garden,
   Sighing the Autumn wind vanishing goes,
Behold now, how close to us dreams are approaching—
   Love, it is time for repose!

List, how the leafage in raindrops all tearful
   Trembles and wails for a sorry defeat,—
All that was ours, that we once proudly boasted,
   All, was a glittering cheat.

Dark as a funeral pall hanging over,
   Fluttering clouds in their mockery close;
Sighing within us is silenced our singing—
   Love, it is time for repose.

Deceitful from heaven's fair emerald rainbow,
   Soft borrowed glamour of moonbeams doth woo;
Since even you to my faith were disloyal,
   Love, my false Springtime were you!

Soon will the sunbeams last radiant shining
   Trackless be hurled where the Autumn wind blows,
Slumber enmeshes my soul and the darkness—
   Love, it is time for repose!

FOFANOW.

THE BEGGAR

There stood a beggar asking alms
   By the cathedral gate,
His face bore torture marks of life—
   Pale, tired, blind—like fate.

Thin, tired, pale and blind he begged
  A crust of bread alone,
And some one pausing, placed within
  His outstretched hand—a stone.

And even so I asked your love,
  I brought my dreams, my life—the while
Unto my passion you replied
  Only with your cold smile!

FOFANOW.

WITH ROSES

Darling, accept my bunch of perfumed roses;—
  Because in royal beauty and in freshness sweet
They dared to rival you,—I cut them down and bound
  The criminals and brought them to your feet.

From the Georgian of Prince Tschawtschawadze.

THE STARS

With joy in your heart and a smile on your lips
  You admired the soft Southern night,
And do you know when your beautiful eyes
  Were remarked, all the stars at the sight
Were put out and turned faint in the skies?

This morning they brought their complaint to the sun—
  "In ether a star quite unknown!
If to-night this same comet shall shine
  Whose radiance extinguished our own,
We must all, our old splendor resign!"

And sadly the sun made them answer,—"Alas!
  Before her, I am pale at high noon;—
See, to-day all is rainy and cold,
  'Tis the trace of defeat seen so soon,
'Tis the trace of eclipse you behold!"

* * * * *

O happy the being whose life from afar
  Shall be lighted by such a lode star!

From the Caucasian of Prince Oberlaine.

WHISPERS AND THE TIMID BREATHING

Whispers and the timid breathing,
　Nightingale's long trill,
Silver moonlight and the rocking
　Of the dreaming rill;
Nightly light and nightly shadow,
　Shadow's endless lace—
Neath the moon's enchanted changes
　The Beloved's face.
Blinking stars as flash of amber,
　Snowy clouds on-rush,
Tears and happiness and kisses—
　And the dawn's red blush!

FROM "FÊTE CHENCHINE."

Fête Chenchine, so-called, has no rival in impressionistic effects. The above without a verb is a good instance of his peculiar caprice.

THE TALES OF THE STARS

The stars of beauty, the stars of purity,
　Have whispered their wonderful tales to the flowers!
The satiny petals have smiled as they heard,
　And trembled the emerald leaves 'mid their bowers.
But infatuate flowers deep drunken of dew
　Repeated these tales to the light swaying breeze—
Rebellious winds listening swift caught them up
　And sang them o'er earth, o'er the mountains and seas!
Now, as the earth under Springtime's caresses:
　With her verdant tissue is covered once more,
All my madly passionate soul overflows
　With dreams of the stars and their radiant lore!
And throughout these days of my sorrow and toil,
　Through these nights of my loneliness, darkness and rain—
Stars wondrous and radiant, I give back to you,
　Your ethereal fancies again!

FOFANOW.

ONE DEAREST PAIR OF EYES I LOVE

One dearest pair of eyes I love!
  Entranced my heart beneath their spell—
Clearer than clearest ray they are,
  But where they are—I will not tell!

Through silk of wondrous lashes soft,
  Their burning beams are flashing bright,
Upon my knees, a slave I kneel—
  Before those miracles of light.

The storm is growing in my soul,
  Tempest of pain and happiness—
I love one dearest pair of eyes,
  But whose they are—I'll not confess!

GIPSY SONG.

A GIPSY SONG

Pile of embers in the darkness,
  Sparks expire as they fly—
Night conceals us from the passing,
  On the bridge we'll say good-by!

At the parting, shawl of crimson
  Cross my shoulders thou shalt lace,
At an end the days swift passing,
  Met within this shaded place.

In the morning, with first splendour,
  All my life compelled to rove—
I shall leave with other gipsies
  Seeking happiness and love.

How does fate foretell my future?
  Who, to-morrow by my side,
O'er my heart will loose with kisses
  Knots by thy dear hand fast tied?

Flash of embers in the darkness,
  Sparks expire as they fly—
Night conceals us from the passing,
  On the bridge we'll kiss good-by!

POLONSKY.

AT LAST

No word,—not e'en a sigh, my darling!
  Together now the silence keeping;
In truth as o'er some grave stone leaning
  The silent willows low are weeping,
And drooping o'er it so are reading—
  I read in thy tired heart at last,
That days of happiness existed,
  And that this happiness is past.

PLESTCHEEFF.

BY AN OPEN WINDOW

So sultry is the hour I throw the casement wide,
  Fall on my knees beside it in the gloom,
And cowering before me lies the balmy night,
  Wafted aloft the breath of lilac bloom.
The nightingale her plaint from a near thicket sobs,
  I listen to the singer, share the woe—
With a longing for my home within me waking,
  The home I looked on last so long ago!
And the nightingales of home with their familiar song!
  And lilacs in my childhood gardens fair!
How the languors of the night possess my being,
  Restoring my lost youth on perfumed air!

THE GRAND DUKE CONSTANTINE.

WITH THE GREATNESS OF GOD

With the greatness of God all my heart is on fire!
  Such a beauty to earth does He lend—
He created eternity for our desire,
  To our torment has given an end.

NADSON.

THE POET

Ne'er have I sung in idle hours of dreaming,
With verse harmonious and sweet-voiced rhyme,
I have sung only when in tempest raging
My soul was shaken by a power sublime!
For each thought I have suffered and been troubled,
No dream creation painless from me torn,
The blessed lot of Poet not seldom seeming
A cross intolerable to be borne!
Oft have I sworn to evermore keep silence,
To mingle and be lost among the crowd,
But when the winds once more their strings are sweeping—
Aeolian harps must ever cry aloud;
And in the Spring the flooding streams on-rushing
Must downward plunge into the vale below,
When from the rocky peaks' high towering summits
The sun's warm rays have melted off the snow.

NADSON.

TO THE MUSE

Take from thy brow the laurel—cast it forth!
  May it in dust lie 'neath thy feet;
The blood-flecked thorn crown hurl away—
  As witness of thy pain alone 'tis meet!

NADSON.

A FRAGMENT

Hark! The storm petrel shrieks!
              Reef the sail canvas fast!
See, the Spirit of Storm with wildest commotion
Has to heaven's arched vaulting his coronal pressed,
While his heels dam the flood gates of ocean!
Furious storm-cloud his undulent drapery,
Girded round with the lightning wide flashing;
O'er the sea's leaden billows from his threatening hand
The thunderbolts are sent crashing!

NADSON.

IN MAY

To you,—you beggars in the forests proud,—
To pastures free, my hasting foot returns!
The May is come! It smiles and laughs aloud—
For Love's desire, freedom's bliss, it yearns.
Erased the marks of city slavery,
Here where the sun gleams gold through azure hours—
Here wrests the spirit from all bondage free,
The fields grown green and the syringa flowers!

Storms only, brought my youthful morning red,
And night of soul and wilderness of pains—
All in my breast is hushed and numb and dead,
The pulsing fever stopped within my veins;
Yet here, where Nature winds a wreath for me,
The arms stretch forth,—the weary glance devours—
And the arrested soul exults and sings,
The fields grow green and the syringa flowers!

NADSON.

IN MEMORY OF N.M.D.

Slumber soft,—oh thou my heart's beloved!
Death alone can bring eternal rest,
And in death alone 'neath tearless lashes
Shall thine eyes forever close be pressed;
In thy grave, no more with fevered doubting
Shall thy golden head tormented be,
In thy grave alone, thou'lt never long for
All that life so cruel robbed from thee.

Through the grass, white yet thy coffin shining—
O'er thy grave the cross is looming white,
As in silent prayer unto the heavens
Mournful gleaming through the cold blue night.
Now with tears my eyes are overflowing,
Hotter tears I ne'er before have wept—
All the bitter sorrows I have suffered
In one sobbing cry together swept.

Spring across the fields will be returning
With her silver nightingales, ere long—

Through the dusky nights of silence piercing
E'en thy grave with her inspiring song,
And the lindens whispering, will murmur—
Breathless die away, and sighing cease,
But thou—slumber soft my heart's beloved,
Death alone can bring eternal peace!

NADSON.

AT THE GRAVE OF N.M.D.

Forsaken am I now anew,
Night's sombre wings o'er me descending,
As tearless, meditating, dumb—
Above thy grave's low mound I'm bending.
Naught offers recompense for thee,
No hopes console or fears betray—
For whom now live I in this world?
For whom on earth now shall I pray?

NADSON.

IN DREAMS

In my dreams I saw heavens bespangled,
  With silvery stars all adorned,
And pale green sorrowing willows
  Drooping low o'er the pale blue pond.
I saw in syringa embowered
  A cottage, and thou my heart's Dove—
And bowed was thy little curly head,
  My beautiful sad pale Love!

Thou wert weeping, the teardrops shining
  Were flowing from thy yearning gaze,
For love the roses wept also,
  For joy sobbed the nightingale.
And every tear found consoling—
  A greeting from near and from far,
The garden was lit by a glow worm,
  Enraptured the heavens a star!

NADSON.

THE OLD GREY HOUSE

Thou hospitable old grey house,—A greeting unto thee!
  With thy red ochre roofs,—vine trellised o'er;
The gardens fair laid forth in blooming luxury,
The fields in glinting beads of dew stretched endlessly,
  Beneath the sun's fresh kiss a gilded floor!

A silvery ribbon through the flowering green—
  The icy billows of the river foam,
Above her clay-white strand are verdant arbours seen,
Spun o'er with leafage, through the waking land between,
  And where the azure river's currents roam.

Prattling, the river lisps of love and of repose—
  And in the distance shimmers, faintly dies;
A flower, secret listening as its message flows,
A roguish kiss of gratitude in fragrance blows,
  While beckoning stars smile from the silent skies.

I greet thee, home and mother! Joys now charm anew
  That I believed but once to me were given;
Thee I forsook,—and now my last expiring view
Turns back from fruitless conflict to thy vision true,
  Love, no more mine, nor hope nor peace of heaven!

Mother and home, I greet thee! O caress thy child
  Whom weariness, regret, despair assail—
With sighing of thy groves in the soft wind beguiled,
With sunbeams of thy Springtime smiling fair and mild,
  And with the liquid song of nightingales!

Let me once only weep in the assurance blest
  That I am not girt round with human scorn,
Let me but sleep once more upon thy gentle breast,
Forgetting in my childish, deeply-dreaming rest
  The loss and failure of my life forlorn!

NADSON.

CALL HIM NOT DEAD

Call him not dead,—he lives!
              Ah you forget
Though the pyre lies in ruin the fires upward sweep,

The string of the harp is broken but her chords still weep,
The rose is cut but it is blooming yet!

NADSON.

BRIEF BIOGRAPHICAL NOTES

ALEXANDER SERGJEWITSCH PUSHKIN was born at Moscow, May 26, 1799. His first poetical influence came from his nurse who taught him Russian tales, legends and proverbs, and to whom, with loving recognition, he was grateful to the end of his life. His grandmother and this nurse taught him to read and write. In his seventh year he began the study of foreign languages; German, French,—which was as his mother tongue to him,—and mathematics, which he hated. At nine the passion of reading possessed him and he devoured his father's library, which included the French erotics, Voltaire, Rousseau, and the Encyclopedists. His own first poetical work was indeed written in French. In 1811 he was sent to the school then just opened, at Tzarskoe Selo near Petersburg. Here, however, he learned little, the students being more interested in drinking bouts and platonic relations with barmaids and actresses; in spite of which the art of poetry was worshiped and Pushkin with others among his friends published a journal in manuscript that circulated their own contributions. He was later graduated from the Alexandrovsky Lyceum, the highest and most splendid civil school of that time, and entered the department of Foreign Affairs. Although he retained his entire sympathy with the poetic brotherhood, he now frequented the salons of the titled aristocracy and gave himself up to the vortex of luxurious society. Because of his political satires and too free opposition to the government, he was sent away from Petersburg in 1820, and attached to the Governor of the South Russian Colonies. Here he fell ill and went to the Caucas for recovery. It was in the Crimea that he learned to know and wonder over Byron. He remained three years in Kischinew,—in the service chiefly of wine, women and cards. In 1823 he went to Odessa as attaché of the General Governor Count Woronzow, whom he pursued with biting epigram,—until in 1824 the poet of "Russlan and Ludimilla" was removed from the service and banished to his mother's estates by order of the Tsar Alexander I.

These two years of unwilling retirement worked mightily upon the soul of Pushkin so filled with storm and stress. He struck off the chains of Byron and steeped himself in Shakespeare; writing at this period his drama of Boris Godunow. Nicholas First amnestied the poet and recalled him to Moscow, instituting himself censor of all future work; likewise placing Pushkin under the all-powerful Chief of Police Count Benkendorff, from whom Lermontoff later had also so much to suffer. In 1829 Pushkin went to the Caucas and with the Russian army to Erzum. In 1830 he inherited from his father the management of But Boldino, where he finished "Onegin," and three other dramas. In 1831 he was married at Moscow to Natalie Nikolajewa Gontsharowa, whose beauty had for three years held him in her toils. In the same year he was appointed to the foreign office again. In 1833 the poem was published that won him his fatal commission. Pushkin fell, as did Lermontoff later, a victim of the envy and hatred of high society. At this time many responsible positions were held in Russia by Frenchmen who had fled the terrors of the revolution. Such a French émigré was D'Anthes, who pursued the wife of Pushkin with his compromising attentions, until at a ball the poet was almost forced to challenge him. The pistol duel, that Count Benkendorff with cunning foresight did nothing to prevent, took place June 27, 1837. In two days the poet was free from his tormentors forever. He was buried in the Swatjatorgorische cloister and statues have been erected to his honor at Petersburg, Moscow and many other cities throughout Russia. His service to Russian literature can only be compared with that of Dante for Italy,—since there was practically no Russian poetry before Pushkin and he may be said to have created the Russian language as it is spoken to-day.

MICHAIL JURJEWITSCH LERMONTOFF was born October 14, 1814, at Moscow. From his father he inherited the love of brilliant society, from his mother the love of music and an unusually sensitive temperament. When he was but two and a half years old his mother died and he became the idol of his grandmother, by whom he was spoiled, until the wilfulness of youth became the arrogance and domineering quality so distinguishing his maturity. Being a delicate child, his grandmother took him at the age of ten to the Caucas,—which he deeply loved ever after. In 1827 he was placed in the Adelige Pension at Moscow, having been previously much influenced by a German nurse who inspired him with a love of German legend and poetry, and also by his tutor, an officer in the Napoleonic guard, who had taught him French. Up to 1831 he was under the German unfluence [Transcriber's note: sic] in literature, but then he came under the influence of Byron, and from this time he was never free of the impression of the poet so congenial to his own spirit and nature. In 1830 he was matriculated by the Moscow University as a student of moral and political science. In 1832 he went to what is now the Nicolai Military school in Petersburg, where he wrote his censurable and erotic poems that were passed about by thousands and won an immense popularity with the jeunesse doré of the time, but which were regarded as discreditable by the more serious and thoughtful society. In November, 1832, he was appointed Second Lieutenant in the Life Guard Hussar regiment, and the young poet now plunged into the vortex of society life as Pushkin had before him. In 1836 appeared his "Song of the Tsar Ivan Wassiljewitsch,"— a truly classical achievement in the record of literature. In 1837 came the poem on the death of Pushkin, that stirred the aristocratic world and caused his banishment to the Caucas by the Emperor Nicholas I. In April of the year 1840 he was again banished to the Caucas for his duel with the son of the historian de Barante, where he distinguished himself by his valor in conflict with the Tscherkes. In February of 1841 we find the poet again at Petersburg, where the second edition of his masterpiece, "A Hero of Our Own Time," was just appearing. Yet toward the end of April again he was obliged to leave,— this time through the influence and hatred of the Countess Benkendorff. For the third time he went to the Caucas in exile. Here in Petigorsk he was forced into close relation with one Major Nikolai Solomonowitsch Martynow,—whom he did not spare from his well deserved scorn. Aroused by the local society that pursued the poet with hatred and envy, Martynow challenged him at a ball. The seconds, as also the entire city, expected a harmless outcome only, especially as Lermontoff, as was known to his adversary, had declared he should shoot in the air. He held his hand high with the pistol stretched aloft; Martynow approached, aimed, fired, and silently the poet fell dead. Thus his own lament for Pushkin came to be worthily written for himself—

"The murderer contemptuous gazing
Did steadfastly his weapon aim—" etc., etc.

At the foot of the Machook mountains, July 27, 1841, in the twenty-seventh year of his age, the poet died. After a year the body was claimed by his grandmother, who lived at this time in the Pensa district, and his remains were removed to be fitly honored in the family village of Tarchany. In connection with the tragedy, it is pitiful to remember that his grandmother wept herself blind over the death of the poet.

COUNT ALEXIS CONSTANTINOWITSCH TOLSTOY was born at Petersburg on the 6th of September, 1817. At the age of six weeks he was taken away from the city to Little-Russia, by his mother and maternal uncle, who was distinguished in Russian literature under the pseudonym of Anton Perowskij. By this uncle he was brought up, enjoying a singularly happy and unclouded childhood. Being an only child he played much alone, living in his dreams and imagination and early developing a love for poetry. At the age of eight or nine years he was taken by his parents to Petersburg where he was presented to the heir to the throne, and allowed to play with his children. The good will shown him at that time he never lost throughout his entire life. The year following he was taken to Germany, and while in Weimar was permitted to visit Goethe, which made a lasting impression upon him. Up to the age of seventeen when he took his examinations for the University at Moscow, he lived both in Russia and abroad. After the death of his uncle, who made him his heir, he became attached, by the wish of his mother, to the Russian Mission at Frankfort. Later he returned to enter the Second Division of the Chancellery of His Majesty. At the time of the coronation of Alexander Second at Moscow, he was appointed to become His Majesty's aide de camp; an honor he declined, not caring for a military career. He was afterward made Chief Master of the Royal Hunt, a position he held until the day of his death. From the age of sixteen he had always written poetry, but not until 1855 did he begin to publish his lyrics and epics in the journals. His passion for poetry was extended toward all other forms of art. At thirteen years of age he made his first journey through Italy,—to Milan, Venice, Florence, Rome and Naples, and his soul grew large with enthusiasm for every manifestation of beauty, so that upon his return to Russia he was really homesick for Italy. He said himself that it was solely due to his passion for hunting that his poems were written in the major key,—while those of so many of his countrymen were written in the minor. Count Tolstoy died on the 28th of September, 1875, at his estates in the government of Tshernigow, where he lies buried.

His most important works were a romance, a dramatic poem, Don Juan,— and the dramatic trilogy, The Death of Ivan the Terrible, Tsar Fedor Ivanowitsch and Tsar Boris.

APOLLON NIKOLAJEWITSCH MAIKOW was born June 4, 1821, at Moscow. His father was a painter; his brothers had rendered important service to Russian literature in history and criticism. As a boy he was instructed in the literature of Russia by the afterward famous Gontscharow. At the age of fifteen he began to write verse. His original intention was to become a painter, but the weakness of his eyes and his increased devotion to poetry decided him otherwise.

He studied jurisprudence at the University of St. Petersburg for several years, and his final collection of poems was published in 1842, which was greeted with enthusiasm by the famous critic Belinsky. In the same year, using the gold he received from the Emperor Nicholas I, he went abroad. He spent nearly a year in Italy, heard lectures at the College de France and the Sorbonne during his stay in Paris, and spent some time in Prague. For a time he served in the Ministry of Finance and from 1852 in the Foreign Censorship office at Petersburg; being President of that office at the time of his death which occurred in March, 1897.

NIKOLAI ALEXAJEWITSCH NEKRASSOW was born in November, 1821, in a village of a Polish province. His father married the daughter of a Polish magnate against the opposition of her parents. The marriage turned out unhappily. There were fourteen children and the poet always thought of his mother as a saint and his father as a tyrant,—which appears in several of his lyric poems. His childhood was spent in Greschenewo where the family had inherited an estate. He was sent to the government school or gymnasium, only until the fifth class. At sixteen he went to Petersburg to pursue a military career by the will of his father. His desire for knowledge drove him toward the University, but his father refused his every request, and during his student years he went hungry very often. He wrote vaudevilles for the Alexander theatre under an assumed name, and not until 1840 published his first volume of verse. In his fortieth year he brought out an anthology of Russian poets that was sufficiently successful to give him a living. In his fiftieth year his health seemed failing, and he went abroad to Italy, where the disaster seemed happily averted. The journal with which he had been connected being now suppressed, he became connected with another for two years. In December, 1877, he died, widely mourned and called "the singer of Russian folk song."

IVAN SSAWITSCH NIKITIN was born October 3, 1824, at Woronesh. Though his life was poor in external circumstances, it was all the richer within. His best biography is his own work, "From the Diary of a Seminarist." His life opened under rather auspicious influences, for his father owned a candle factory and was so prosperous that his business amounted yearly to a hundred thousand roubles. A shoemaker taught the precocious boy to read, and he was put to school at first in the local school, but this was exchanged in 1841 for the Seminary. Both here and at home he was, however, more cudgelled than educated, and his soul was threatened with suffocation in scholastic confusion. Only one consolation was always his; literature and poetry. While here the first great misfortune befell. His father's business failed, the house was turned into an inn and Ivan, instead of attending the University, as he had expected, was obliged to sell candles, not only in his father's shop, but as that was soon taken from him, even in the market place. After a few months his mother died and his father sacrificed his last remaining possessions for drink. He insulted and even attacked his son, bidding him leave his house, and the poor boy was compelled to render the most menial service to all. For ten long years this condition lasted, yet Ivan remained a poet!

In 1853 at the opening of the Crimean war, his patriotic hymn, "To Russia," appeared in the Woronisher *Times*. This was received with applause and a circle of intelligent men gathered about him who were friendly and helpful in their disposition toward him. In 1856 Count Alexis Tolstoy, the great poet, prepared a volume of his poems for publication and the imperial family sent him costly gifts. His condition became improved and by 1859 he had amassed a capital of two thousand roubles, with which he opened a book-shop, hoping to enlighten the darkness of his country. To this ideal he gave all his strength and his money. In 1860 Nikitin went to Petersburg and Moscow to establish connections with the leading publishing houses; from which no small literary acquaintance arose. In the Spring of 1861 he suffered from a throat trouble which developed into bronchial tuberculosis of which he died on October 16, 1861. His trials with his father and those caused by his father's extreme intemperance were considered to have greatly hastened his lamented death.

CONSTANTINE MICHAILOWITSCH FOFANOW was born at Petersburg, May 30, 1862. He is not a highly educated man, and is now living, after a series of misfortunes, happily surmounted, at Gatschina.

SEMIJON JAKOLOWITSCH NADSON was born at Petersburg, December 26, 1862. On his father's side he was of Hebrew extraction. His grandfather had formerly embraced the orthodox faith, and his father, from whom he inherited his musical talent, died in an asylum, in the extreme youth of the poet. His mother, after contracting a second marriage, which ended unhappily, died at the age of thirty-one, of consumption. The boy learned to read and write at the age of four, from an old servant. At nine he had read widely. In 1875 he suffered from religious doubts, and even lost his faith in humanity, but his violin and Nature were still of unfailing support even in this crisis. Before her death his mother had placed him in the second Cadet Corps as a "pensionnaire." At first he did well, but soon he began to neglect his school work for poetry. A poem of his soon appeared in print, and that same year he fell in love with a girl of sixteen who died with rapid consumption; the M.D.B. of his poems. Smitten by this blow, he left the school and went to the Pawlonische Military School. Here he contracted a lung trouble and was sent to the Caucas. He remained there a year, but was always haunted by thought of the military career before him, for which he was morally and physically unfit. His dear dream of the University could not be realized, and on his return he went again to the military school for two years of camp life and maneuvres. In September, 1882, he was made second lieutenant of a Caspian regiment and stationed at Kronstadt. Already the young poet was making himself known through the journals, and in 1884 he left off his hated military service. For a short time he was connected with *Die Woche*, but already signs of tuberculosis had appeared and he found that a journey abroad was indispensable. On the funds raised by influential friends, and the prize awarded him by the Russian Literary Society, he was enabled to go abroad this same year, accompanied by a friend of his mother. He went to Wiesbaden, Nice, Mentonne, Berne, was operated upon three times for the trouble in his foot, but to no avail. His only desire became to return to his native land to die. In the summer of 1885, he went back to Kiew, where for a time he seemed to improve and was able to write some criticisms for the journals. When his left lung gave out, he moved to Yalta in the Crimea. Here he received the glad news that the Academy had given him the Pushkin award of five hundred roubles.

In November he bequeathed all he had written to the literary fund; whose Nadson capital now amounts to more than two hundred thousand roubles from the sale of his works. He died in January, 1889. His body was brought to Petersburg and interred with public honors. His grave, which is near other celebrated Russian writers, is adorned by a bust from the hand of the famous sculptor Antokolsky. His poetry enjoys a popularity beyond that of any one poet in Russian, and has been carried to the eighteenth edition of one hundred and twenty thousand volumes each.

Sketches of the lives of the poets here represented by a single poem are omitted as unnecessary to enjoyment of their work.